Saratoga Springs

A Brief History in Postcards

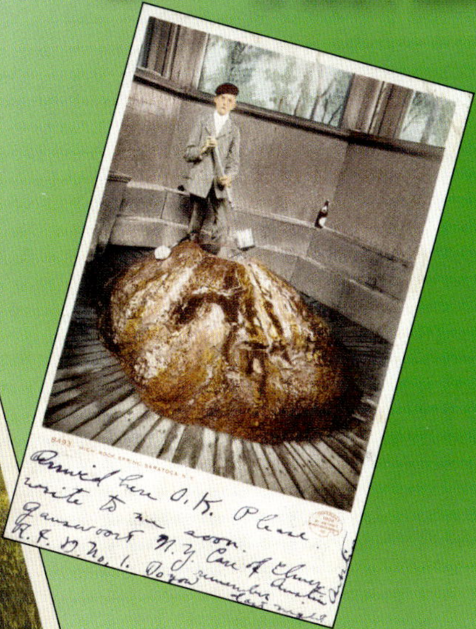

Mary L. Martin and
Nathaniel Wolfgang-Price

Schiffer Publishing Ltd
4880 Lower Valley Road, Atglen, PA 19310 USA

Other Schiffer Books by Mary L. Martin
Bathing Beauties of the Roaring '20s. Mary L. Martin & Tina Skinner.
Greetings from New Orleans: A History in Postcards. Mary L. Martin, Tina Skinner
Hawaiian Fish. Mary L. Martin
Hollywood Homes: Postcard Views of Early Stars' Estates. Mary L. Martin, Tina Skinner, & Tammy Ward
Miami Memories: A Midcentury Journey. Mary L. Martin, Tina Skinner, & Nathaniel Wolfgang-Price
Midget Exhibit: Images from the Heyday of Dwarf Display. Mary L. Martin & Tina Skinner
Naughty Victorians and Edwardians: Early Images of Bathing Beauties. Mary L. Martin & Tina Skinner
Cape Cod Memories: An Illustrated History in Postcards. Karen Choppa & Mary L. Martin
Geisha Women of Japan's Flower & Willow World. Tina Skinner, Mary L. Martin, & Wes Ponder
Greetings from Havre de Grace. Craig David & Mary L. Martin
Hawaii Remembered: Postcards from Paradise. Tina Skinner, Mary L. Martin, & Nathanial Wolfgang-Price
Historic Christmas Art: Santas, Angels, Poinsettia, Holly, Nativity, Children, and More Royalty-free Images on CD. Mary L. Martin & Tina Skinner
Historic Holiday Art: New Year, Valentines, St. Patrick's Day, Easter, July 4th, Halloween, & Thanksgiving. Tina Skinner & Mary L. Martin
Lighthouse Views. Tina Skinner, Mary Martin Postcards
Memories of Memphis: A History in Postcards. Ginny Parfitt & Mary L. Martin

Other Schiffer Books on Related Subjects
Advertising Postcards. Robert Reed
Art Deco Architecture: Miami Beach Poscards. Paul Clemence
Birds of Cape Cod & the Islands in Postcards. Roger S. Everett
Cape May Postcards.
Card Photographs: A Guide to Their History and Value. Lou W. McCulloch
Greetings from Ohio: Vintage Postcards 1900-1960s. Robert Reed.
Miami Beach Postcards.
Mies van der Rohe's Farnsworth House Postcard Book. Paul Clemence
Newport News: A Vintage Postcard Tour. Harold Cones & John Bryant

Library of Congress Control Number: 2006932303

Designed by Mark David Bowyer
Type set in University Roman Bd BT / Arrus BT

ISBN: 0-7643-2594-9
Printed in China

Published by Schiffer Publishing Ltd.
4880 Lower Valley Road
Atglen, PA 19310
Phone: (610) 593-1777; Fax: (610) 593-2002
E-mail: Info@schifferbooks.com

For the largest selection of fine reference books on this and related subjects, please visit our web site at **www.schifferbooks.com**
We are always looking for people to write books on new and related subjects. If you have an idea for a book please contact us at the above address.

This book may be purchased from the publisher.
Include $3.95 for shipping.
Please try your bookstore first.
You may write for a free catalog.

In Europe, Schiffer books are distributed by
Bushwood Books
6 Marksbury Ave.
Kew Gardens
Surrey TW9 4JF England
Phone: 44 (0) 20 8392-8585; Fax: 44 (0) 20 8392-9876
E-mail: info@bushwoodbooks.co.uk

Contents

Cathedral Arch of American Elms, Grand Union Hotel Park.
Greetings from Saratoga Springs.
Robson & Adee, Saratoga Springs, N. Y.
MADE IN GERMANY

Preface

Historic Images Through Postcards

Postcards are said to be the most popular collectible history has ever known. The urge to horde them sprang up with the birth of this means of communication at the turn of the twentieth century and has endured great changes in the printing industry. Today, postcard shows take place every weekend somewhere in the country, or the world, and millions of pieces of ephemera lie in wait for those who collect obscure topics or town views.

Postcards once served as the email of their day. They were the fastest, most popular means of communication beginning in the 1890s in the United States. These timely cards provided a way to send scenes through the mail along with brief messages – a way to enchant friends and family with the places travelers visited, to send local sights, or to share favorite topics of imagery. They even provided the latest breaking news, as images of fires, floods, shipwrecks, and festivals were often available in postcard form within hours of an event. Moreover, mail was delivered to most urban homes in the United States at least twice a day. So someone might send a morning postcard inviting a friend to dinner that evening, and receive an RSVP in time to shop for food.

The messages shared and the beautiful scenes combine to create the timeless appeal of postcards as a collectible. Most importantly, history is recorded by the pictures of the times, moments in time reflecting an alluring past.

Dating Postcards

Pioneer Era (1893-1898): Most pioneer cards in today's collections begin with cards placed on sale at the Columbian Exposition in Chicago on May 1, 1893. These were illustrations on government printed postal cards and privately printed souvenir cards. The government cards had the printed one-cent stamp, while souvenir cards required a two-cent adhesive postage stamp to be applied. Writing was not permitted on the address side of the card.

Private Mailing Card Era (1898-1901): On May 19, 1898, private printers were granted permission, by an Act of Congress, to print and sell cards that bore the inscription "Private Mailing Card." A one-cent adhesive stamp was required. A dozen or more American printers began to take postcards seriously. Writing was still not permitted on the back.

Example of a postcard with an undivided back. Senders could only write the address on this side of the card. Any message needed to be written on the front of the card along with the picture.

Post Card Era – Undivided Back (1901-1907): New U.S. postal regulations on December 24, 1901, stipulated that the words "Post Card" should be printed at the top of the address side of privately printed cards. Government-issued cards were to be designated as "Postal Cards." Writing was still not permitted on the address side. In this era, private citizens began to take black and white photographs and have them printed on paper with post card backs.

Sample of a postcard with a divided back. Senders were allowed to put an address on the right hand side of the postcard and a message on the left side.

Early Divided Back Era (1907-1914): Postcards with a divided back were permitted in Britain in 1902, but not in the U.S. until March 1, 1907. The address was to be written on the right side; the left side was for writing messages. Many millions of cards were published in this era. Up to this point, most postcards were printed in Germany, which was far ahead of the United States in the use of lithographic processes. With the advent of World War I, the supply of postcards for American consumption switched from Germany to England and the United States.

White Border Era (1915-1930): Most United States postcards were printed during this period. To save ink, publishers left a clear border around the view, thus these postcards are referred to as "White Border" cards. The relatively high cost of labor, along with inexperience and changes in public taste, resulted in the production of poor quality cards during this period. Furthermore, strong competition in a narrowing market caused many publishers to go out of business.

Linen Era (1930-1944): New printing processes allowed printing of postcards with high rag content that created a textured finish. These cheap cards allowed the use of gaudy dyes for coloring.

Photochrome Era (1945 to date): "Chrome" postcards began to dominate the scene soon after the Union Oil Company placed them in its western service stations in 1939. Mike Roberts pioneered these with his "WESCO" cards soon after World War II. Three-dimensional postcards also appeared in this era.

About Saratoga Springs

Introduction

On July 27, 1873, on a tour through northern New York State, George Washington and a small party of guest staying at the nearby house of Major General Phillip Schuyler, made their way through the fog-shrouded landscape to see what the locals called the "Salt Springs." Washington and his band became the first tourists to visit the area that would later become one of the most famous resorts in the country. In fact, Washington was also the first to envision a resort at Saratoga Springs. He came away from his visit, his head full of possibilities for such a location. He wrote to several people in the hopes that they would invest with him; however, none were interested. Washington would eventually give up the idea and move on to bigger things.

Unlike Washington, others, like Gideon Putnam – who is credited for much of the early development of Saratoga Springs as a town and tourist center, harnessed the potential of the area and its springs and soon the town of Saratoga Springs was born. By 1787, enough visitors were coming for a local entrepreneur to justify building a tavern; by 1802 there were enough to build the first hotel, Union Hall; and by the 1820s, it was America's leading resort, attracting thousands of tourists. These tourists ranged from ordinary people looking to get away for a while to celebrities including President John Quincy Adams and Joseph Bonaparte, the former King of Spain and the brother of the late Napoleon Bonaparte.

Throughout the eighteenth, nineteenth, and twentieth centuries, Saratoga Springs was the place to be. Health seekers came for the curative powers of Saratoga's springs, which were said to cure all kinds of ailments from gout to asthma. Devotees of music and culture came to see famous artists like John Philip Sousa, Enrico Caruso, and Chauncey Olcott, who came to perform at New York's "summer music capital." New York moguls and captains of industry came for some much needed rest and relaxation. Racing enthusiasts, jockeys, gamblers, bookmakers, and horse breeders and owners came for the Saratoga Race Meeting, while members of high society came to see and be seen. Of course, wherever tourists came, postcards left. Inexpensive and convenient, the postcard was ideal for the traveler, especially one with a busy schedule who did not have a great deal of time to sit down and write a long letter. Small and easy to carry, they fit well into a pocketbook, a suitcase, or an overnight bag. There was room on the back to jot down a quick message, letting everyone back home know you were all right, had arrived safely, and were having a good time. On the front were pictures and scenes of the places you had been to and the things you had seen, excellent visual aids for any trip narrative.

Vintage black and white and hand-tinted postcards paint pictures of a long ago time, showing the sites and scenes that made Saratoga Springs famous. Historical trivia and quoted material from the backs of the cards will add some fun to this overview of one of America's premier resort towns.

Greetings from Saratoga Springs, New York, the Spa City.

Circa 1900s, $5-7

Horse and carriage decorated for the annual Floral Fete and Carnival.

Circa 1900s, $5-7

Though it is noted for its summer life, Saratoga Springs was filled with activity even in the winter.

Cancelled 1911, $2-4

Bankrupt and seriously ill due to throat cancer, former President Ulysses S. Grant and his family moved to this cottage on Mount McGregor near Saratoga Springs on June 16, 1885. He had been contracted by Mark Twain to write his memoirs, which he hoped would provide his family with income after his death.

Cancelled 1908, $4-6

History

Saratoga Springs' history began in the late 1700s with the building of a rough log tavern near High Rock Spring by Alexander Bryan. Bryan had been a double agent, working for both the British and the Americans in the Revolutionary War using his high standing with the British to secure and pass along information about troop movements to the Continetal Army.

Other individuals, mostly farmers and loggers, soon followed Bryan, setting up homesteads throughout the area.

A few years after Bryan built his tavern, another individual who would play a large part in Saratoga Springs' history settled in the vicinity. Though he was interested mostly in lumber, Gideon Putnam, like Washington and Bryan, saw potential in what was around him. Using his lumber profits, he acquired land around Congress Spring. In 1802, he bought a parcel of land across from the spring and built "Putnam's Tavern and Boarding House," later Union Hall and the Congress Hall in 1811. This proved to be a great attraction to the tourists, who could stay next to the famous spring and use it free of charge.

Putnam's hotel combined with the already popular Saratoga springs soon proved to be just what Saratoga Springs needed to begin to grow. With the subsequent rise in population, both seasonal and permanent, Saratoga Springs established itself as a town in 1819 and was incorporated as a village on April 17, 1826. Throughout the following years, Saratoga Springs continued to grow and prosper, with new hotels, boarding houses, homes, churches, and restaurants built to accommodate the steady influx of tourists and permanent residents. The main economic concerns became the exportation of mineral water, tourism, and a thriving health industry centered on the mineral springs.

In August of 1863, one month after the bloody battle of Gettysburg, Saratoga Springs also arrived at a turning point in its own history, its first thoroughbred race meeting. The event was organized by John Morrissey, a former boxer and gambler who would go on to become a Democratic Senator and the owner of one of the most popular gambling establishment in Saratoga Springs. The race meeting was a tremendous success, with two thousand people staying at the United States Hotel alone. With the start of the races, the town became the capital of another faction of the American social elite, the racing set, making Saratoga Springs even more popular.

After the Civil War, Saratoga Springs reached the height of its popularity, playing host to such notables as Diamond Jim Brady, Lillian Russell, and Commodore Cornelius Vanderbilt. The town was now, more than ever, the place to see and be seen.

Despite a racing ban imposed in the early 1900s that caused Saratoga Race Course to shut down temporarily, the town continued to do well. In 1911, Lucy Skidmore Scribner began converting the Young Women's Industrial Club she had opened several years earlier, into the Skidmore School of Arts (later Skidmore College). Also, in 1912, the state of New York passed legislation making the Saratoga springs a state reservation and taking over their ownership. This eventually led to the establishment of another Saratoga Springs landmark, the Saratoga Spa.

During World War II, gasoline and tire rubber shortages made it difficult to transport horses. This, combined with the lack of interest in racing, hit the city fairly hard. A number of landmarks, like the United States Hotel, were demolished because of the lack of business. Visitors still came to visit the mineral springs and the tracks eventually reopened, however the crowds did not possess the size and enthusiasm they once had.

Today Saratoga Springs is once again a thriving tourist destination and sports and racing center. The city is well known for the health-giving qualities of its mineral springs, its summer culture, and its elegant Victorian mansions.

This memorial on Mount McGregor marks the spot where Ulysses S. Grant had his last view of the Hudson River Valley on July 20, 1885, one day after completing his memoirs and three days before his death on July 23.

Circa 1920s, $2-4

Inside Saratoga Springs

The City

When it was incorporated as a village in 1826, the original borders of Saratoga Springs were defined as follows: all land beginning in the center of the highway near the house of Jesse Ostrander (a local farmer) running north to Broadway, and then continuing north on Broadway until it meets the highway which lead from the upper part of the village to the town of Greenfield. Since then the boundaries have been expanded and today encompass over seventy-five square kilometers in Saratoga County, New York.

Much of Saratoga Springs' early development was the work of Gideon Putnam, who had moved to the area in 1789. Having acquired land around Congress Spring, he soon purchased more, laying out a plan for the future development of Saratoga Springs. In a nutshell, Putnam's plan called for one long road, 120 feet wide and one mile long, that would connect the "Upper Village," which had developed around High Rock Spring, to the "Lower Village" around Congress Spring.

Convention Hall was built in 1892 as a headquarters for the numerous conventions that were held in the city each year.

Circa 1900s, $5-7

Though originally viewed with some skepticism by local residents, Putnam's Broad Way soon became the main thoroughfare in Saratoga Springs. Putnam was also responsible for the layout of "lesser" streets like Bath, Congress, and Federal Streets, which were included in his overall city plan. Other streets, like the famous Union Avenue, would be added much later as the city expanded and outgrew its original boundaries.

The Saratoga Springs Hospital.

Circa 1940s, $3-5

The Clark Textile Company's Plant at Saratoga Springs.

Circa 1900s, $6-8

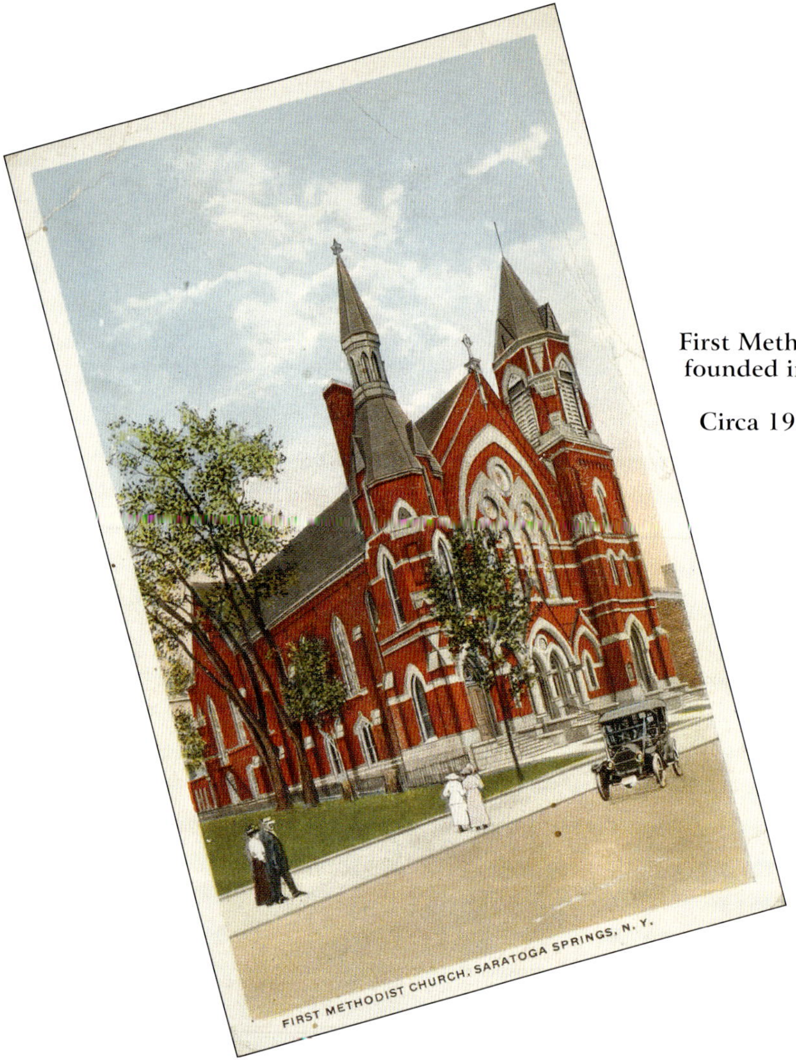
FIRST METHODIST CHURCH, SARATOGA SPRINGS, N. Y.

First Methodist Church, founded in 1831.

Circa 1920s, $4-6

Saratoga Springs, N.

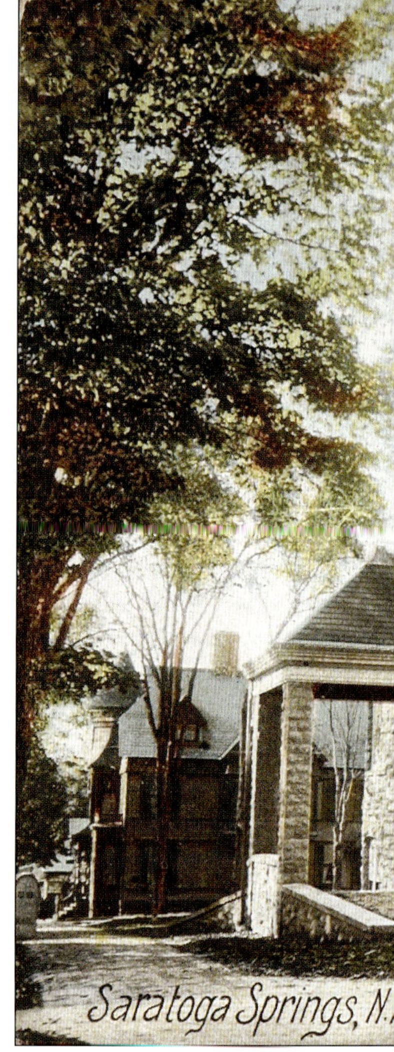

The First Congregational Church of Saratoga Springs was founded in 1865.

Cancelled 1906, $5-7

Shrine at Glen Mitchell.

Cancelled, 1906, $1-3

The Grotto, a shrine located on the grounds of St. Clement's Roman Catholic Church.

Circa 1940s, $1-3

Another view of the Grotto at St. Clement's.

Circa 1920s, $1-3

Skidmore College began as the Young Women's Industrial Club organized by Lucy Skidmore Scribner. The club was chartered as the Skidmore School of Arts in 1911. It was independently chartered as a four-year college in 1922.

Cancelled 1931, $5-7

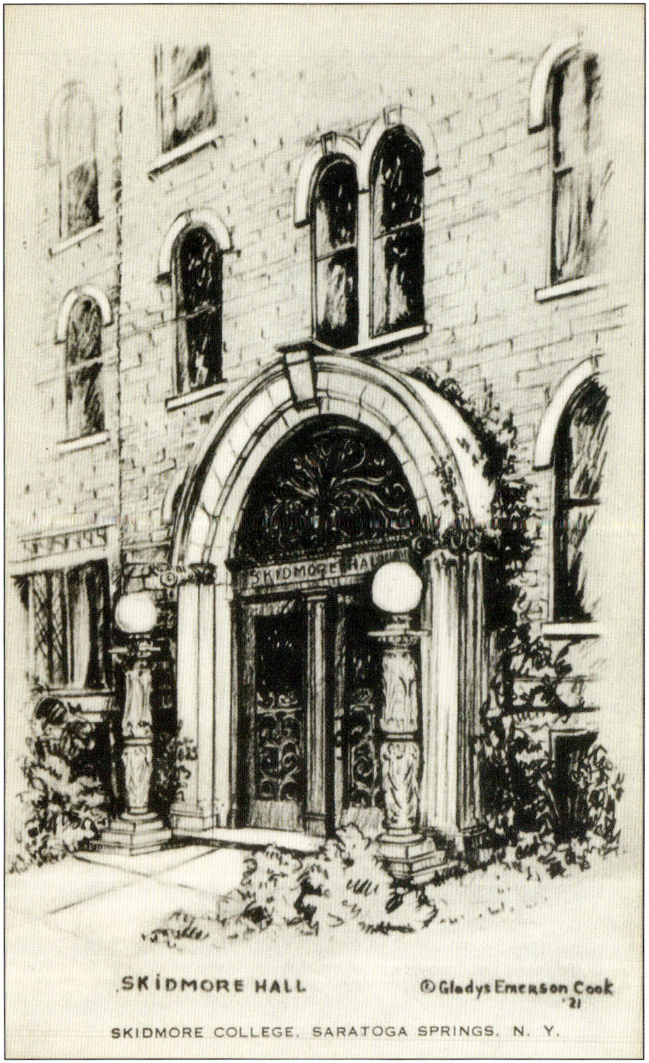
SKIDMORE HALL
© Gladys Emerson Cook '21
SKIDMORE COLLEGE, SARATOGA SPRINGS, N. Y.

Originally chartered as an all-female school, Skidmore College did not accept its first male student into its undergraduate program until 1971.

Circa 1930s, $4-6

MAIN ST

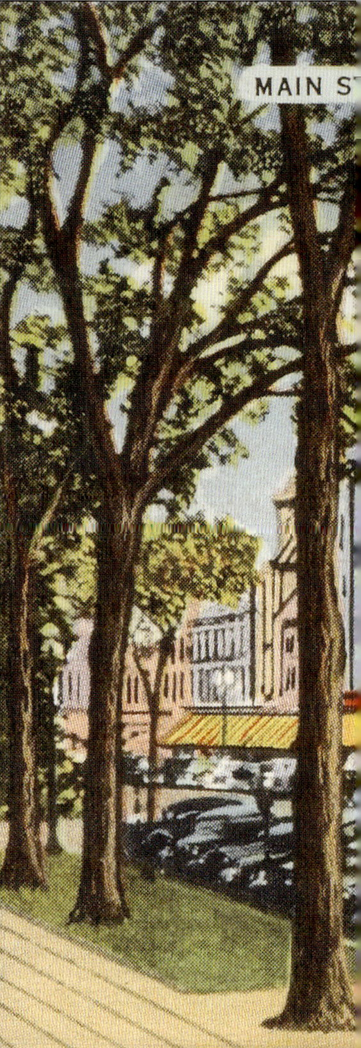

Main Street, as seen from the porch of the United States Hotel.

Circa 1940s, $7-9

View of Broadway, showing the entrance to Congress Springs Park.

Cancelled 1907, $4-6

Right:
Broadway was one of the main thoroughfares in Saratoga Springs. At any time of the day, well-dressed tourists and residents could be seen strolling up and down the street.

Circa 1900s, $4-6

Broadway, Saratoga, N. Y.

Broadway was laid out by Gideon Putnam, the individual responsible for most of the early development of Saratoga Springs.

Circa 1900s, $3-5

Another view of old Broadway.

Circa 1900s, $5-7

Early Broadway was 120 feet wide and almost a mile long. The thoroughfare ran from the Upper Village at High Rock Spring and the Lower Village at Congress Spring.

Cancelled 1907, $5-7

Looking west down Broadway.

Circa 1900s, $6-8

Broadway and the front of the Grand Union.

Circa 1900s, $6-8

Elm trees along North Broadway.

Circa 1900s, $3-5

Looking down North Broadway.

Circa 1910s, $3-5

Originally East Congress Street, Union Avenue was redeveloped by Warren W. Leland, the manager of Union Hall (Union Hotel) in the 1860s.

Cancelled 1901, $4-6

Union Avenue began at Broadway and ran for three and a half miles past Saratoga Race Track to Saratoga Lake.

Circa 1900s, $4-6

Because of the large amounts of dust stirred up by the frequent traffic on Union Avenue, it was the first street in Saratoga Springs to be paved.

Circa 1900s, $4-6

Summer Houses

In the late 1860s, during Saratoga Springs' postbellum boom, many of the town's summer visitors began moving away from the hotels and building elaborate summer cottages (i.e. mansions). While many of these summer homes did not last longer than their owners, a few still survive today. The best examples can be found on North Broadway, Union Avenue, Circular Street, and Lake Avenue, creating one of the largest collections of private Victorian architecture on the East Coast.

Summer home of Chancellor "Chauncey" Olcott, an actor, singer, and songwriter who was a frequent performer in Saratoga Springs during the summer concert season.

Circa 1900s, $5-7

Olcott named his summer home, Inniscarra, after the town of Inniscarra in County Cork, Ireland.

Circa 1900s, $5-7

Situated on Clinton Street, Inniscarra was built in the early 1900s and is still standing today.

Circa 1940s, $3-5

The gardens at Inniscarra.

Cancelled 1906, $3-5

Right:
The Old Oaken Bucket.

Circa 1920s, $3-5

218573
THE OLD OAKEN BUCKET, CHAUNCEY OLCOTT'S GARDENS, SARATOGA SPRINGS, N. Y.

Right:
Hylande, the home of G.N. Ostrander.

Circa 1920s, $4-6

More of the gardens at Inniscarra.

Circa 1920s, $2-4

97-40
"HYLANDE," RESIDENCE OF G. N. OSTRANDER, SARATOGA SPRINGS, N. Y.

Even before the Civil War, Saratoga Springs was known as a gathering place for members of the social elites, many owning summer homes along Union Avenue and North Broadway.

Cancelled 1939, $5-7

Parks

In the mid-1820s, John Clarke, a developer and businessman, bought Congress Springs and the land around it. Shortly afterwards, he remodeled the land turning the swampy grounds into one of the most famous and celebrated public places in Saratoga Springs, Congress Park. Well-known to both residents and visitors, Congress Park has been called by some historians "a microcosm of Saratoga Springs." On any given day, provided the weather was nice, anyone from the lowliest chambermaid at the Grand Union to the wealthiest tourist could be seen strolling around Congress Park. The park also became noted for being one of the venues for the Saratoga Springs summer music season, featuring such notables as John Philip Sousa and the Sousa Band, Enrico Caruso, Chauncey Olcott, and Gartland's Tenth Regiment Band. Saratoga Springs was also home to one of the country's largest private parks, Woodlawn Park, which was part of the estate of Judge Henry Hilton. Tours were permitted through the estate, however they were severely limited and were usually accompanied by guards.

Love Lake in Woodlawn Park, at one time it was thought to be the largest private park in the country.

Circa 1900s, $4-6

Woodlawn Park was part of the estate owned by Judge Henry Hilton. The public was allowed to visit Woodlawn Park, however the visits were monitored and regulated by carding and guards.

Circa 1900s, $4-6

Wayside, a private residence located in Woodlawn Park.

Circa 1900s, $4-6

Cottage belonging to financier Clarence Mackay. He and his wife Katherine maintained a number of homes in New York, including one in New York City and another in Long Island.

Cancelled 1911, $5-7

In 1961 Woodlawn Park was purchased by J. Erik Jonsson, a trustee of Skidmore College, and is now the home of the college's Jonsson Campus.

Circa 1900s, $2-4

Old Man Saratoga is a rock formation in the Petrified Gardens three miles outside of Saratoga Springs.

Circa 1940s, $1-3

Dancing pavilion in Kayderass Park. The Park's name comes from the Kayderosseras Trail, a trail used by Mohawk Indians when they visited the springs.

Circa 1900s, $1-3

OLD MAN SARATOGA—A NATURAL ROCK FORMATION 325

SA-H2629

PETRIFIED GARDENS, 3 MILES WEST OF SARATOGA SPRINGS, N. Y. ROUTE 29

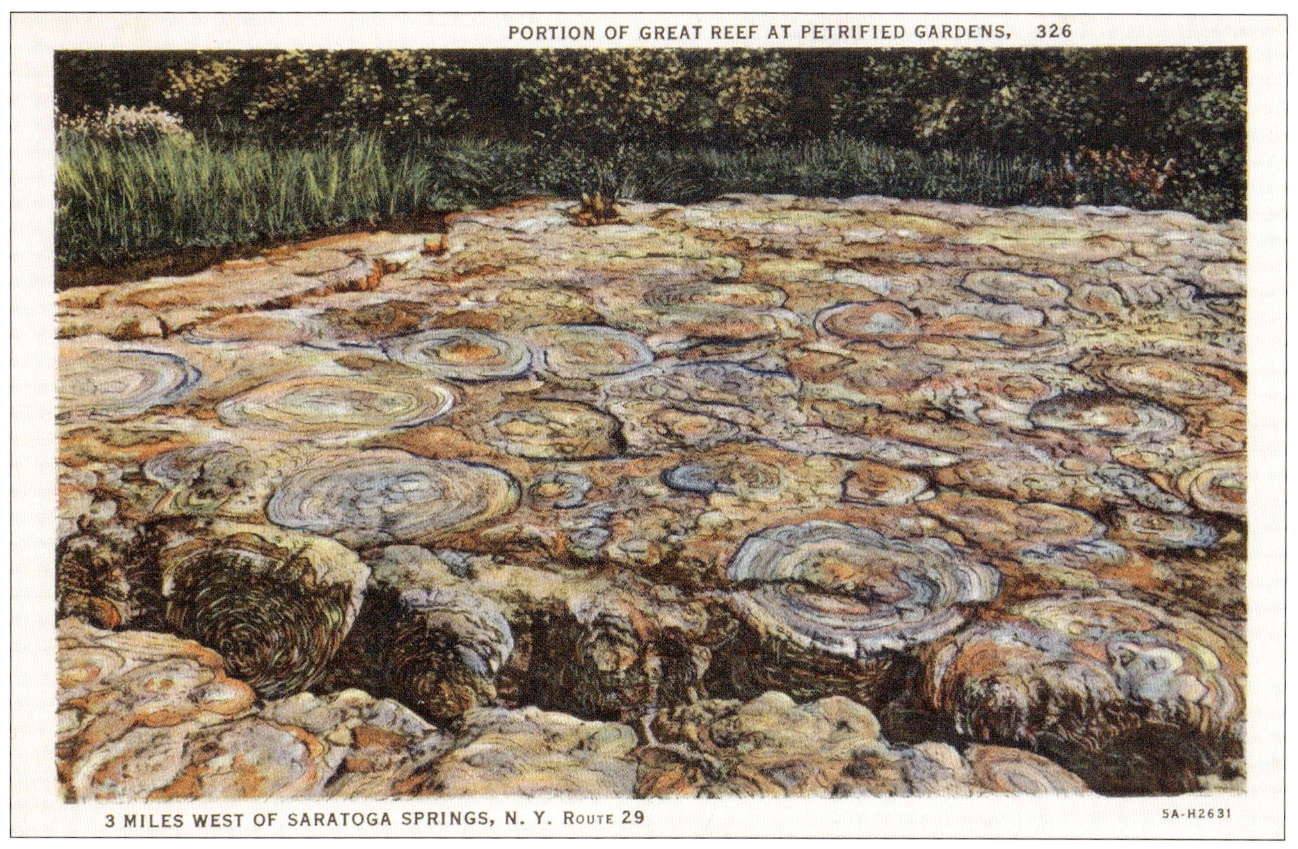

Petrified wood is formed when wood and other plant materials become covered with sediment. Mineral rich water then flows through the silt, replacing the organic matter with minerals, leaving a cast of the original shape.

Circa 1940s, $1-3

110 feet tall, eighteen feet around, and 250 years old, the Iroquois Pine is one of the largest and oldest white pines in America.

Circa 1940s, $1-3

Joseph Bonaparte, the brother of Napoleon Bonaparte, came to Saratoga Springs. He visited Saratoga Springs five times during his exile. During one of these trips, he tried to buy High Rock Spring for $20,000 but his offer was refused.

Cancelled 1913, $3-5

Congress Springs was discovered in 1792 by Nicholas Gilman, a congressman from New Hampshire, and was named in his honor. It is one of the most popular springs in the city and is still active to this day.

Cancelled 1913, $5-7

John Clarke, a Saratogan entrepreneur and developer, purchased the land for Congress Park in the mid-1820s, shortly after purchasing Congress Spring.

Cancelled 1913, $4-6

John Morrissey built the Canfield Casino in 1870. After his death, it was bought by Charles Reed and Albert Spencer and then sold to Richard Canfield, who managed the Casino until 1911. Canfield sold it and the surrounding grounds to the city, which would, in turn, make it part of Congress Park.

Cancelled 1908, $5-7

Saratoga. Club House Dining Room
Printed by Louis Glaser, Leipzig, Germany.

Each of the stained glass windows in the ceiling of the Canfield Casino Dining Room features a representation of one of the signs of the zodiac.

Circa 1900s, $4-6

Left:
Under the management of Charles Reed and Albert Spencer, the Canfield Club became known as the Saratoga Club House. The dining room was built in 1903 when Richard Canfield owned the Casino.

Circa 1900s, $5-7

When the city of Saratoga Springs reopened the Casino in 1912, it became a place for people to gather, to drink spring water, play games (gambling was not allowed), sit, read, and smoke.

Cancelled 1904, $4-6

After he purchased the Casino, Canfield also bought the property along its north and east sides and built the Italian Gardens.

Cancelled 1915, $2-4

Along with the Casino, the Italian Gardens were also sold the to the city in 1911.

Cancelled 1920, $2-4

Bandstand and pond in Congress Park.

Circa 1900s, $2-4

Like the other springs in the city, the waters of Congress Springs were reported to have healing properties.

Circa 1900s, $2-4

Congress Spring Lake.

Circa 1910s, $2-4

Congress Park was extremely popular with both residents and visitors. On any given day Saratogans of every class and social standing, as well as numerous visitors from abroad, would gather and mingle in the park.

Circa 1910s, $2-4

The Grand Union Hotel, as seen from Congress Springs Park.

Circa 1920s, $3-5

During the summer Congress Park was the site of public concerts with performances by such notable groups as John Philip Sousa and the Sousa Band and Gartland's Tenth Regiment Band.

Cancelled 1907, $2-4

The Italian Fountain in Congress Park, the two tritons at either end are known as "Spit" and "Spat."

Circa 1940s, $1-3

Besides public fountains, visitors to Congress Park could also purchase spring water from "dipper boys," boys who sold spring water by the dipperful.

Cancelled 1909, $2-4

A typical scene in Congress Springs Park.

Circa 1910s, $2-4

The Saratoga Springs War Memorial was dedicated in 1931 all the Saratogans who served and died in World War I

Circa 1910s, $1-3

Visiting Saratoga Springs

Hotels

Saratoga Springs' first hotel was built by Gideon Putnam in 1802, a three story building he called "Putnam's Tavern and Boarding House." The locals called it "Putnam's Folly." However foolish the locals thought the idea was, it worked. Visitors came by the hundreds; so many that Putnam began construction on another hotel in 1811, the Congress Hall Hotel. Unfortunately, Putnam never lived to see the completion of the Congress Hall. He was seriously injured in a construction site accident and never fully recovered. His wife and children continued on, eventually completing the Congress Hall and renaming the boarding-house Union Hall.

It was places like the Grand Union, Congress Hall, and the United States Hotel (built in 1824) that helped to change the concept of what a hotel was to the American traveler. No longer were hotels just places for bed and board, but destinations in and of themselves with nightly parties or balls and plenty of activities for guests to do during the day. It was here that residents and visitors could meet and mingle with friends and associates in an elegant and gracious setting.

These hotels also made their marks on American architecture by being some of the first buildings in the country to feature piazzas (colonnaded porches). Reproduced by Putnam on the front of the Congress Hall, they were soon featured on hotels throughout the town. There guests could sit outside and enjoy the weather, be able to see the street, be seen by those in the street, and still have a sense of privacy since the piazzas were elevated above street level.

Of the many hotels in Saratoga Springs, the Grand Union, the United States, and the Congress Hall were seen as the largest and most elegant hotels, not only in the town but in the country. They remained in operation for many years, until the decrease in patronage brought on by anti-gambling legislation and a suspension of racetrack operations during World War II spelled their end.

In 1853 a diner at the Moon Lake Lodge complained that the French fries prepared by the Lodge's head chef George Crum were too thick, too soggy, and not salty enough. Frustrated and annoyed by the complaints, Crum prepared another batch of French fries, slicing them wafer-thin, pouring salt over them, and frying them to a crisp. The "Saratoga Chips," as they came to be called, became an instant hit and were a local delicacy for many years.

Circa 1900s, $5-7

Right: In 1802 Gideon Putnam began construction on Putnam's Boarding House and Tavern, Saratoga Springs' first hotel. It was eventually renamed Union Hall after Putnam's death in 1811.

Circa 1900s, $5-7

Grand Union Hotel—Saratoga.

SARATOGA, N.Y. Grand Union Hotel Court.
Took dinner here
Pete

The management and ownership of Union Hall was taken over by the Leland Brothers in 1864. That same year the hotel burned down in a fire. When it was rebuilt in the 1870s, it was re-christened the Grand Union Hotel.

Circa 1910s, $4-6

Left:
The hotel court at the Grand Union. By 1863, Union Hall was the largest hotel in the city and one of the largest in the country.

Cancelled 1907, $4-6

During their ownership of the Grand Union, the Leland Brothers made a number of improvements to the building. One of these was a three story, three hundred foot long piazza pictured here.

Circa 1900s, $4-6

Elm trees in the Grand Union Hotel Park.

Cancelled 1903, $4-6

By 1876, the Grand Union Hotel consisted of five stories with room to accommodate 2,000 guests.

Circa 1900s, $3-5

GRAND UNION HOTEL, SARATOGA

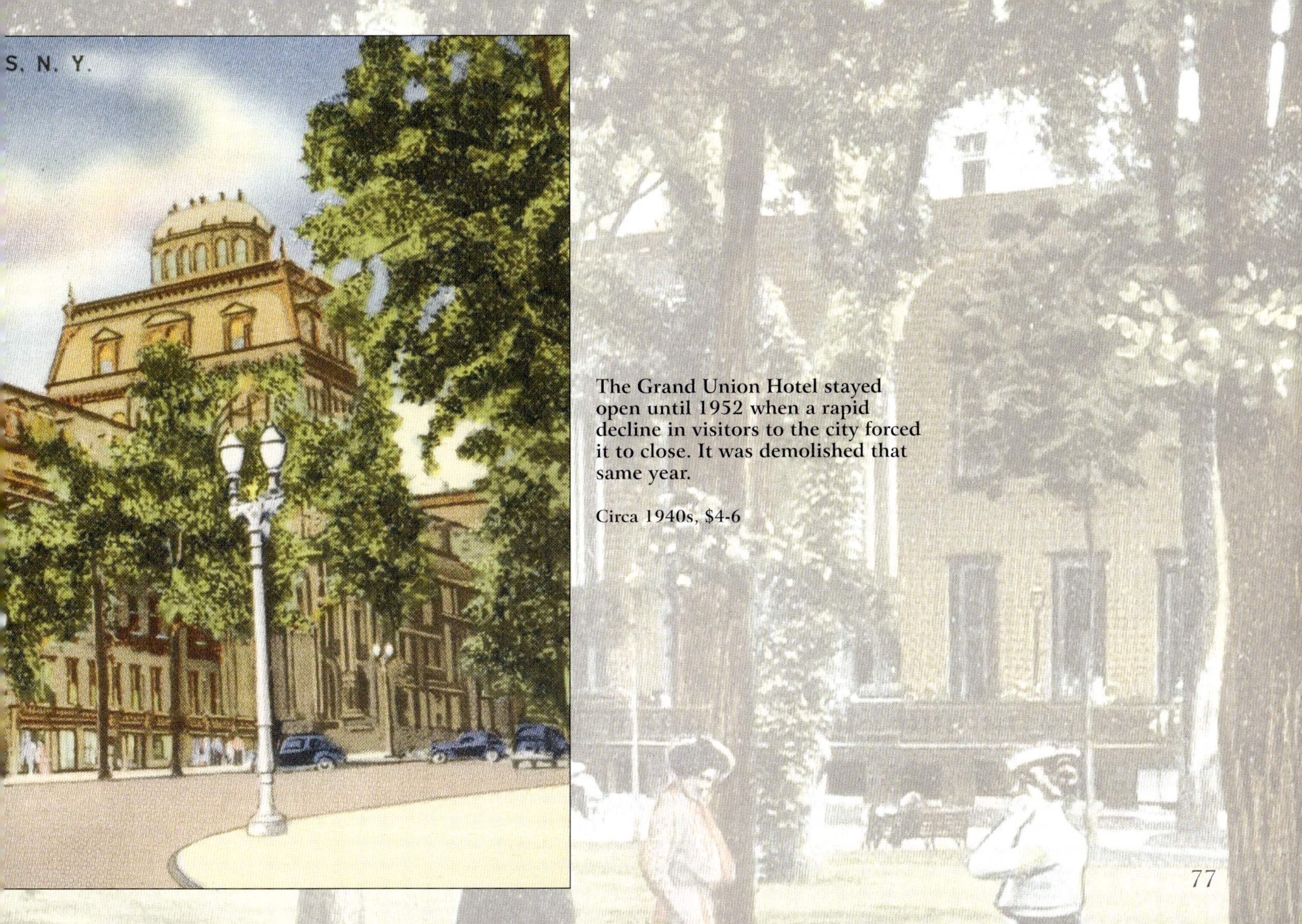

The Grand Union Hotel stayed open until 1952 when a rapid decline in visitors to the city forced it to close. It was demolished that same year.

Circa 1940s, $4-6

The Worden Hotel, located on the corner of Division Street and Broadway.

Cancelled 1909, $5-7

Another view of the Worden Hotel.

Cancelled 1908, $5-7

WORDEN HOTEL.
SARATOGA SPRINGS, N. Y.

Also located on Broadway, the United States Hotel was one of the top three hotels in Saratoga Springs.

Circa 1900s, $4-6

Left:
The Worden Hotel was known particularly for its bar, which was said to be one of the classiest in Saratoga Springs.

Circa 1940s, $5-7

The first United States Hotel was built in 1824; after a fire in 1865 it was reopened on June 20, 1874.

Circa 1940s, $4-6

Interior court of the United States Hotel. The main building of the hotel had 768 single rooms and sixty-five suites with one to seven sleeping rooms and a parlor and private bath in each. The hotel also featured 917 cottages, all located in one building on the hotel grounds.

Circa 1920s, $4-6

The hotel itself stood five stories high and covered seven acres.

Cancelled 1905, $3-5

The Congress Hall Hotel was also built by Gideon Putnam. Unfortunately, Putnam died after a construction accident in 1811.

Circa 1910s, $6-8

While it was not the largest of the hotels in Saratoga Springs, Congress Hall was considered by many to be the most architecturally pleasing.

Circa 1900s, $6-8

Left:
After Putnam's death and the hotel's completion, management of the Congress Hall was taken over by Guert Van Schoonhoven, who purchased the hotel from Putnam's estate.

Cancelled 1906, $4-6

3661—
American Adelphi Hotel, Saratoga, N. Y.
SOUVENIR POST CARD CO., NEW YORK.

The Windsor Hotel employed an all-German wait staff.

Cancelled 1906, $6-8

Left:
Built in the "off-season" between 1876 and 1877, the American Adelphi Hotel was owned and operated by William McCaffrey, a former conductor on the Rensselaer and Saratoga Railroad, and Seymour Ainsworth, one of Saratoga Springs' most prominent builders. It is the only remaining Victorian hotel still in operation in Saratoga Springs.

Circa 1900s, $5-7

EXCELSIOR SPRING HOTEL
Excelsior Springs Hotel,
Saratoga Springs, New York

Like many of the hotels in Saratoga Springs, the Excelsior Spring Hotel was built near a mineral spring.

Circa 1940s, $4-6

Left:
The Excelsior Springs Hotel.

Circa 1940s, $5-7

Yaddo

In 1881 Spencer Trask purchased a large portion of land in Saratoga Springs. His first child, Alanson, had died suddenly the previous year in his home in Brooklyn and he believed that the distance would help him and his wife, Katrina, deal with the grief. They had spent a considerable amount of time in Saratoga Springs before and the area was familiar and comfortable to them. The land Spencer Trask purchased had belonged to the family of Jacobus Barhyte, and was already famous for the quality of the trout that lived in the ponds and the delicious trout dinners served in the tavern nearby. The Trasks named their estate "Yaddo," following the suggestion of their daughter Christina as the opposite of the word "shadow." It was believed that Christina came up with the word after overhearing her parent's discussion in which they said their life had been overshadowed by the death of Alanson some years earlier.

They remodeled the existing house on the estate, turning it into a massive Queen Anne style mansion and reshaping the grounds to resemble the Italian gardens that they had seen while traveling abroad. Unfortunately, Spencer and Kristina's days of happiness were severely numbered and tragedy came to Yaddo with the deaths of the Trask's three remaining children in 1888 and in 1889. These tragedies were followed by the destruction of the estate's house in a fire in 1891.

The house was eventually rebuilt. Upon its completion the Trasks resumed their lives, returning to entertaining an eclectic mixture of guests, as they had before. However, the question remained: What was to become of the estate once Spencer and Kristina passed on? The solution came to Kristina in 1900 in what she would later describe as a vision. Yaddo would become "...a permanent home to which may come from time to time for rest and refreshment, authors, painters, sculptures, musicians, and other artists both men and women few in number and chosen for creative gifts and besides and not less for the power and the [will] and the purpose to make these gifts useful to the world." The idea was formalized in 1900 and a corporation was set up to oversee the financial and legal matters pertaining to the creation and maintenance of the retreat.

Management of the estate eventually fell to George Foster Peabody following the death of Spencer in 1909 and the death of Kristina in 1923. A financier and philanthropist, Peabody had long been a friend to the Trasks (as well as being Kristina's husband the last year of her life). He shared their vision and appointed Elizabeth Ames to be the estate's executive director. In 1926, Ames opened the retreat and welcomed the first group of Yaddo artists. Since then, Yaddo has been home to over 5,500 artists, including Leonard Bernstein, Sylvia Plath, Truman Capote, Aaron Copeland, and Langston Hughes.

Spencer Trask and his wife Katrina bought the land for their estate in 1881. They named it "Yaddo" after a suggestion given by one of their daughters.

Circa 1900s, $3-5

3096 NELSON AVE. ENTRANCE TO "YADDO," SARATOGA SPRINGS. N. Y.

The entrance to Yaddo on Nelson Avenue.

Cancelled 1914, $1-3

Trask purchased the Yaddo estate following the death of his first child, Alanson, in the family's Brooklyn home in 1880. He believed that the distance of Yaddo from Brooklyn would help his wife deal with her grief over the loss.

Circa 1910s, $2-4

Right:
The Trask Chapel.

Circa 1900s, $3-5

Saratoga Springs, N.Y., Trask Chapel at Yaddo.

At present, Yaddo consists of 400 acres near Saratoga Race Track.

Cancelled 1920, $1-3

This Yaddo Mansion was built in 1893, after a fire had destroyed the original building two years before.

Circa 1900s, $4-6

Aware of his wife's budding artistic inclinations, Spencer Trask made sure that the plan for the new mansion had a space in the tower (situated on the front of the house) for his wife to work.

Cancelled 1906, $4-6

The gardens at Yaddo were modeled after the classical Italian gardens the Trasks had seen when they were abroad in Europe.

Circa 1920s, $1-3

Rock Garden, Yaddo Park, Saratoga Springs, N. Y.
14707

Work on the construction of the gardens began shortly after the Trasks purchased the estate and ended in 1899. The gardens were given, as a gift, by Spencer to Katrina.

Circa 1940s, $1-3

Left:
Spencer Trask picked out most of the stones in the Rock Garden from his own quarry.

Cancelled 1925, $1-3

Amateur dramatists with an interest in medieval society and culture, Spencer and Katrina would often stage elaborate scenes, pageants, and masques in the gardens.

Circa 1940s, $1-3

Located on the second terrace of the gardens, this sundial is inscribed with a poem written by Henry Van Dyke, a poet who was a friend of the Trasks, which reads "Time / is / Too slow for those who wait / Too swift for those who fear / Too long for those who grieve / Too short for those who rejoice / But for those who Love Time is / Eternity." Around the edge of the sundial is inscribed: "Hours Fly, Flowers Die, New Days, New Ways, Pass By, Love Stays."

Circa 1940s, $1-3

After the deaths of the Trasks, Yaddo and the surrounding estate became a center for the arts. Since then, the gardens have gained the nickname, "the Poet's Corner of Yaddo."

Circa 1900s, $2-4

Today the Yaddo gardens are maintained and cared for by the Yaddo Garden Association, which was formed in 1991.

Cancelled 1921, $1-3

Saratoga Lake

Saratoga Lake is located four miles southeast of Saratoga Springs in the lower part of the Adirondack Mountains. The body of the lake is eight and a half miles long, one and a half miles wide at its widest, and ninety-six feet deep at its deepest. It is part of a watershed encompassing an area of 244 miles, is fed by Keydorass Creek, and empties out in Fish Creek.

Greetings from Saratoga Lake.

Circa 1940s, $2-4

Located four miles southeast of Saratoga Springs in the lower part of the Adirondack Mountains, Saratoga Lake is well known throughout the area as an excellent place for bass fishing, boating, and water-skiing.

Circa 1940s, $1-3

Moonlight over Saratoga Lake.

Circa 1940s, $1-3

The lake itself is eight and a half miles long and one and a half miles wide at its widest point.

Cancelled 1906, $1-3

According to a Mohawk legend, the Great Spirit would sink the canoe of anyone who broke the silence of Saratoga Lake.

Cancelled 1946, $1-3

In 1874 the fourth annual regatta of the Rowing Association of American Colleges was held on Saratoga Lake. This was an event that marked the beginning of national interest in college sports.

Circa 1910s, $2-4

Professional sculling was also very popular during the late 1800s, with races being held on the lake as early as 1865.

Cancelled 1908, $2-4

For those who enjoyed boating there was a pubic dock and private marina built along the lakeshore.

Circa 1940s, $3-5

Ryall's bathing beach.

Circa 1940s, $3-5

Saratoga Race Course

Of all that makes Saratoga Springs famous – the exuberance of its summer society, the elegance of its Victorian architecture, and the healing powers of its mineral springs, perhaps the most well-known of these is the Saratoga Race Course.

The racecourse was the idea of John Morrissey, a former boxer who was already running one of the most successful gambling establishments in Saratoga Springs. Morrissey had, coincidentally, also organized the first thoroughbred race meeting in Saratoga Springs, which had run from August 3 to August 6, 1863.

The race was held at the Saratoga Trotting Course. While the race drew a tremendous crowd, the track conditions were poor, there was no grandstand, no good views of the track, the turns were too sharp, and the course was too short. Seeing these inadequacies, Morrissey sent out a call for subscriptions to fund a jockey club and to build a better race course. A number of well-to-do racing enthusiasts – among them Commodore Cornelius Vanderbilt and William R. Travers (the Saratoga Association's first president and the individual after whom the Travers Stakes are named), John R. Hunter, and Leonard James – responded and within two hours $10,600 had already been collected.

Morrissey chose ninety-four acres outside the city across from the Trotting Course. Construction began soon after and was finished in that same year. The track itself was a mile long, with two stretches each a quarter of a mile long, and forty-three feet wide, except for the front stretch, which was sixty-three feet wide. The track also featured a marvelous grandstand, which was two hundred feet long by thirty feet wide and was capable of seating two thousand people, who could see the racetrack perfectly from every seat.

The first race run at the new Saratoga Race Course was held on August 3, 1864, and drew a crowd of five thousand spectators. Admission to the new track cost fifty cents, plus an additional dollar to watch from the grandstand or from a carriage. For ten dollars, spectators could buy a badge that would gain them admittance to the grandstand and the quarter stretch for all five days of the meeting.

Saratoga Race Course still stands today and still appears roughly the same as it did back in 1864. It is the oldest major sports venue in North America and one of the oldest still in continual use. Since 1864, it has been the home of the Travers Stakes, the oldest thoroughbred race in the United States. The Saratoga Race Meeting begins the last week in July and ends Labor Day. The Race Meeting has been held in Saratoga every year since 1864, with the exception of 1943, '44, and '45 because of the travel restrictions and fuel and personnel shortages brought on by World War II.

Grand Stand, at Saratoga Race Course, Sar

Horse racing in Saratoga Springs began around 1825, with races held on the roads and streets both inside and outside of the city.

Circa 1910s, $7-9

Owned by General Stephen Sanford, Mohawk II, pictured here coming down the track, ran his first race at Saratoga Race Course in 1901. He would go on to win the Saratoga Special four years later.

Circa 1900s, $9-11

Two hundred feet long and thirty feet wide, the Saratoga Race Course grandstand could sit two thousand people and offered an unobstructed view of the track from any angle.

Cancelled 1916, $9-11

Early entrance fees to the Saratoga Race Course cost fifty cents for general admission, one dollar for a seat in the grandstand, one dollar to park a carriage on the grounds and watch from there, or ten dollars for a badge allowing access to the grandstand and quarter stretch for all of the five days' races.

Circa 1910s, $8-10

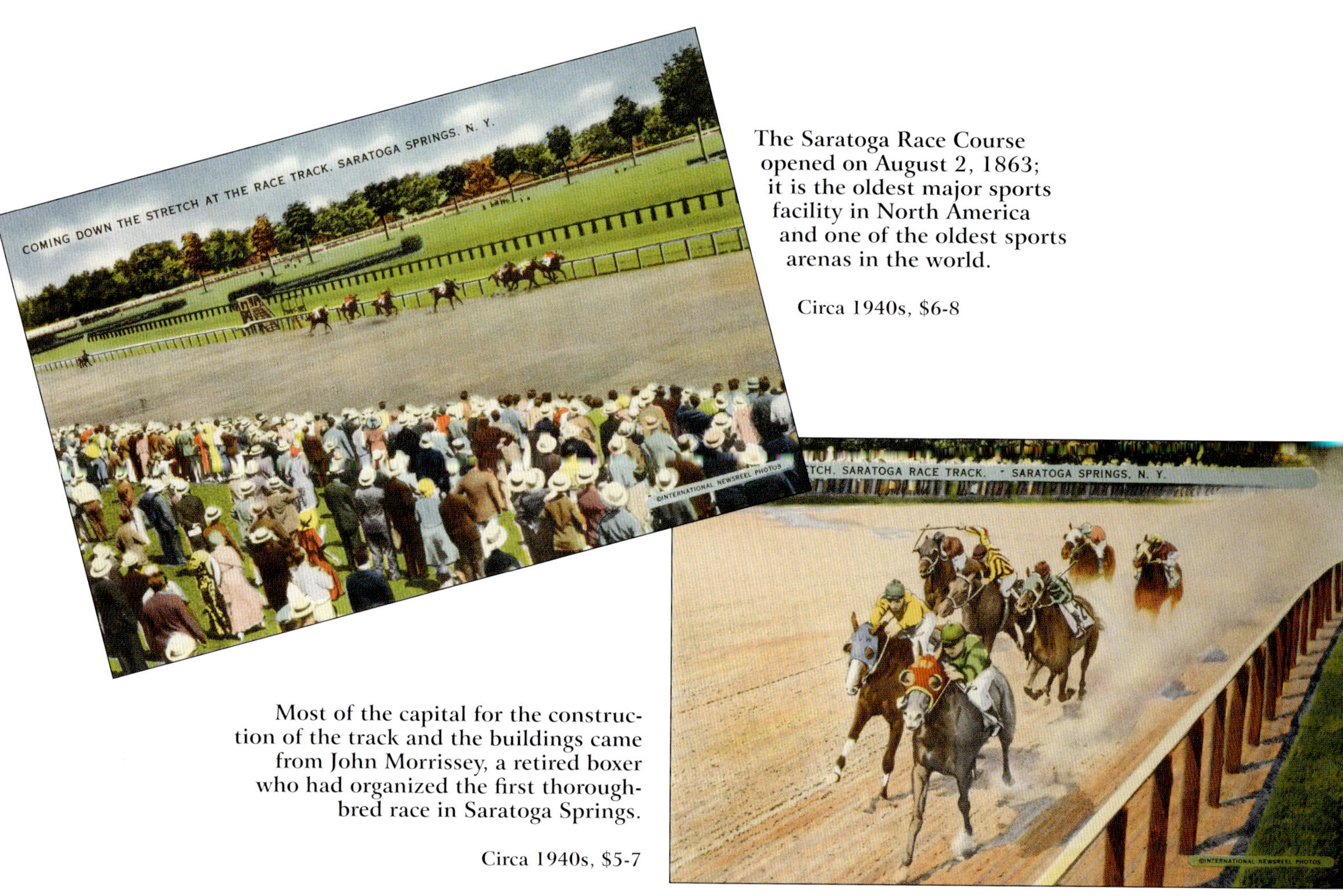

The Saratoga Race Course opened on August 2, 1863; it is the oldest major sports facility in North America and one of the oldest sports arenas in the world.

Circa 1940s, $6-8

Most of the capital for the construction of the track and the buildings came from John Morrissey, a retired boxer who had organized the first thoroughbred race in Saratoga Springs.

Circa 1940s, $5-7

Because of all the "upsets" that have taken place there over the years, Saratoga Race Course has been nicknamed the "Graveyard of Favorites."

Circa 1940s, $5-7

Since 1864, Saratoga Race Course has been the home of the Travers Stakes, the oldest thoroughbred horse race in the United States.

Cancelled 1908, $10-12

Right:
Beginning in August, the Saratoga Race Meeting was the highlight of the social season for many of the country's social elite.

Circa 1910s, $9-11

Club House at Saratoga Race Track, Saratoga, N. Y.
69-4

Steeplechase races are also held at the track and usually take place on the inner turf course.

Circa 1940s, $2-4

Right:
Cornelius Vanderbilt Whitney founded the National Museum of Racing and Hall of Fame in 1950 to honor the achievements of American thoroughbred racing horses, as well as those of individual jockeys and trainers. Originally located in the former Canfield Casino, it has since moved to a newer location across from the Race Course.

Cancelled 1951, $3-5

Saratoga Historical Society & National Museum of Racing, Inc., Saratoga Springs, N. Y.
77979

Springs

The mineral springs at Saratoga Springs have long been valued for the health-giving properties they possess. Even before the Europeans came to the area it was a favored retreat for the Mohawk and the Iroquois, who had originally come to the area to hunt the game that was drawn there by the high salt content of the spring waters. Soon after, they discovered the springs and came to value their medicinal properties, believing the springs to be a gift from the Great Spirit.

The springs themselves result from a geological phenomenon, a fault that is caused by the growth of the Adirondack Mountains. The fault allows carbonated mineral water to escape from deep beneath the ground and rise to the surface. For water to be considered mineral water it must be carbonated, have a slight degree of radioactivity, and have at least fifty grains of salt per gallon.

When Europeans began settling in the area, they too came to realize the healing powers of the Saratoga springs, drinking from and bathing in the springs. Supposedly, the first European to visit them was Sir William Johnson, the British Superintendent of Indian Affairs, who was carried there by his friends among the Mohawks for treatment of an old thigh wound.

As Saratoga Springs grew, the popularity and reputation of the springs grew as well. More and more visitors came to cure ailments ranging from jaundice to dyspepsia. Word of the Saratoga springs was carried even further by the distribution of Congress Water from the famous Congress Spring. It was said that there was not a town in the country that did not stock it and not a ship on the ocean that did not have it in its stores. In fact, Congress Water was one of first products to be distributed nationally in the United States and was exported to Europe long before Louis Perrier leased the spring in Vergèze, France.

In 1908, in order to keep the springs from being pumped dry, the state of New York passed a law to limit the amount of water pumped from the Saratoga springs and in 1911 passed legislation passing ownership of those wells to the state. Famous springs in Saratoga Springs include Congress, Cosea, High Rock, Hathorn, Island Spouter, and Orenda Springs.

An aerial view of Saratoga Spa.

Circa 1940s, $3-5

Built in 1930, the Lincoln Baths is the only bathhouse in Saratoga Spa that is still in operation today.

Circa 1940s, $3-5

A commission headed by financier and presidential advisor Bernard Baruch developed the Spa.

Circa 1940s, $3-5

The Roosevelt Baths, named after Franklin Delano Roosevelt, was the most modernly equipped of all the bathhouses.

Cancelled 1939, $4-6

Right:
The Simon Baruch Research Institute was dedicated to medical research and the exploration of the medicinal properties of the springs' mineral water. The Institute is named after the hydrotherapist who first advocated the development of a health spa in Saratoga Springs.

Circa 1930s, $4-6

THE SIMON BARUCH RESEARCH INSTITUTE, SARATOGA SPA, N. Y.
4

Those who stayed at the Spa usually took rooms at the Gideon Putnam Hotel, named after the first developer and hotel owner of Saratoga Springs.

Cancelled 1938, $4-6

Three of the ten springs found inside Saratoga Spa were housed inside the Hall of Springs.

Circa 1940s, $4-6

From the back: "The great hall is 160 feet long, 70 feet wide, its ceiling arching 38 feet above the variegated floor. Marble pillars and huge chandeliers of silver and crystal feature the majestic splendor of this, one of the most notable public buildings in America."

Circa 1940s, $4-6

Figures representing Earth and Water symbolize the natural phenomenon of the mineral springs at Saratoga Spa.

Circa 1930s, $2-4

Victoria Pool is located in the interior court of the Saratoga Spa Recreation Building.

Circa 1940s, $3-5

Part of the park's original construction, Victoria Pool was the first heated pool built in the United States.

Circa 1930s, $2-4

Geyser Lake.

Circa 1910s, $1-3

Saratoga Springs, N.Y., Geyser Lake.

Vista in Geyser Springs Park.

Cancelled 1908, $3-5

Island Spouter, a spring found in Geyser Springs Park. Geyser Springs and Orenda Springs are the two most visited springs in the city.

Circa 1940s, $1-3

Island Spouter Springs first emerged in the early 1900s; its plume has been known to travel up to fifteen feet in the air.

Cancelled 1938, $1-3

The mound around Island Spouter Springs is made up of tufa, a formation of calcium-carbonate that forms by precipitation from water with calcium content. The formation is still growing at a rate of two inches per year.

Circa 1930s, $1-3

Coesa Springs. Saratoga Springs is home to the only actively spouting geysers east of the Mississippi River.

Circa 1920s, $3-5

In 1912, New York Governor Charles Evan Hughes approved a law naming eight hundred acres in Saratoga Springs a state reservation and transferring ownership of the springs to the state government.

Circa 1940s, $5-7

It is estimated that, by the mid-1800s, up to seven million bottles of Saratoga Springs Mineral Water were being bottled and shipped around the world.

Cancelled 1914, $7-9

A stonemason who was working on the foundation for the Congress Hall Hotel's ballroom discovered Hathorn Spring No. 1 in 1868.

Cancelled 1909, $5-7

The newly discovered spring was named after H.H. Hathorn, the owner of the Congress Hall Hotel.

Circa 1900s, $5-7

To be classified as mineral water, a body of water must have carbonation, at least fifty grains of salt per gallon, and contain a small amount of radioactivity.

Circa 1900s, $6-8

HATHORN SPRINGS, SARATOGA, N. Y.

After its discovery, Hathorn Spring quickly became popular with visiting tourists and health-seekers, even more so than the famous Congress Springs.

Cancelled 1907, $5-7

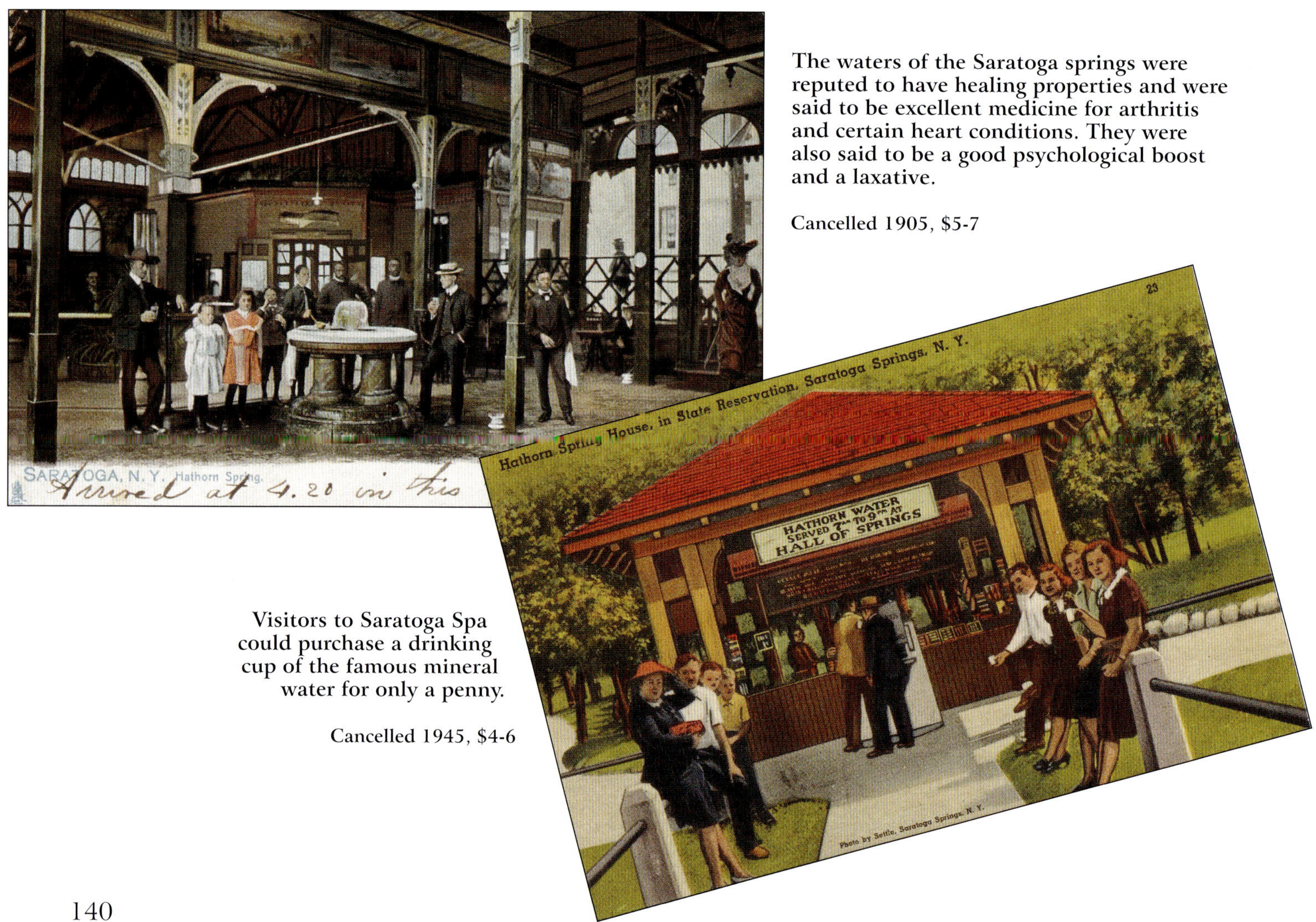

The waters of the Saratoga springs were reputed to have healing properties and were said to be excellent medicine for arthritis and certain heart conditions. They were also said to be a good psychological boost and a laxative.

Cancelled 1905, $5-7

Visitors to Saratoga Spa could purchase a drinking cup of the famous mineral water for only a penny.

Cancelled 1945, $4-6

From the back: "Both on foot, and by automobile, come the constant stream of visitors to Hathorn No. 3 Spring, who partake of these famous waters, not only at the spring itself, but often carry the waters to their homes in jugs and demijohns."

Cancelled 1923, $4-6

Vichy Springs was named after the famous mineral springs of Vichy, France, which are also reputed to have healing properties.

Circa 1910s, $4-6

Saratoga Battlefield

On September 19, 1777, 3,300 British soldiers, 3,900 German mercenaries, and 650 Canadians and Indians under the command of General John Burgoyne advanced in three columns towards an American force under General Horatio Gates. Having learned of this advance, Gates ordered Colonel Daniel Morgan and the 11th Virginia Regiment to intercept two of the columns. The British and the Americans met and exchanged fire at Freeman Farm, which was a mile north of the American camp. The fighting stretched on for three hours until the third column, made up largely of Germans, arrived, forcing the American's to retreat. The British victory was costly, however, and forced Burgoyne and his troops to entrench and to wait for reinforcements from General Clinton.

Both sides of the monument erected at Braymann Redoubt, where General Benedict Arnold rallied the American forces to push back the advancing British during the Battle of Bemis Heights, the second conflict of the Battle of Saratoga.

Circa 1940s, $1-3

Burgoyne waited for three weeks, but the reinforcements never came. Stuck between advancing and retreating, General Burgoyne sent out a troop of 1,500 soldiers and eighty cannons to test the American flank on October 7. Gates responded with a force of three columns under Generals Enoch Poor and Ebenezer Learned and Colonel Morgan, who repeatedly broke the British lines. Before the British could rally, Benedict Arnold (who had been relieved of his command following a quarrel with Gates) rode up to the battlefield and lead General Learned's column against the Germans, who were holding the British center. The Germans broke and the Americans pursued, launching a series of attacks against the British encampments. Arnold led one charge personally, attacking the fortifications at Balcarres Redoubt. Unable to carry forward against the British, Arnold galloped off across the battlefield and joined the final charge of the American forces at Breymann Redoubt.

As darkness fell, the fighting ended and Burgoyne withdrew his surviving men to the Great Redoubt and from there retreated northward until he reached the fortified encampment at Saratoga (now Schuylerville), where he eventually surrendered on October 17, 1777.

Today, the battlefield is located inside the boundaries of the Saratoga National Historical Park. The park was formed in the 1920s due to the efforts of a group of private citizens who came together to form the Saratoga Battlefield Commission. In 1926, the New York State Legislature passed a bill creating the Saratoga Battlefield, which opened in 1927 to a crowd of 160,000 people. It was made a national historical park in 1938, a legislation that was championed by President Franklin Delano Roosevelt, who had frequently taken visiting dignitaries on tours of the battlefield when he was governor of New York.

The Park itself encompasses three separate parts, the actual battlefield where the Battles of Freeman Farm and Bemis Heights took place, the General Phillip Schuyler House in Schuylerville, and the Saratoga Monument located in the village of Victory. Although the name implies otherwise, Saratoga Battlefield is not in Saratoga Springs, but fifteen miles east of the city.

MEMORIAL TO THE UNKNOWN SOLDIERS 21

WHO PERISHED IN THE BATTLES OF SARATOGA, 1777

3A153

This monument was erected by the New York State Chapter of the Daughters of the American Revolution in 1931 and is dedicated to the unknown soldiers who perished in the Battle of Saratoga.

Circa 1930s, $1-3

During the battle, Benedict Arnold was wounded in his left leg. This monument only commemorates his wounding and his role in helping to win the Battle of Saratoga, not Arnold himself, who is still remembered as one of the most infamous traitors in American history.

Circa 1940s, $1-3

Erected by the Saratoga County branch of the Ancient Order of Hibernians, this monument honors Timothy Murphy, a sharpshooter with Colonel Daniel Morgan's 11th Virginia Regiment of the Continental Line. Murphy shot General Simon Fraser, preventing the British forces from rallying and turning the tide of battle in the American's favor.

Circa 1930s, $1-3

Pavilion dedicated to the memory of the Americans who died in the Battle of Saratoga.

Circa 1920s, $2-4

A reproduction of a period blockhouse built by the New York State Department of Conservation in 1927.

Circa 1930s, $2-4

The Memorial was erected in 1927 by the Daughters of the American Revolution and stands on the site of the American Cemetery.

Circa 1930s, $2-4

Building that served as the headquarters for Generals Enoch Poor and Ebenezer Learned and Colonel Daniel Morgan. It was the only building in the battlefield that dates back to the Battle of Saratoga.

Circa 1920s, $2-4

PERIOD HOUSE, BEMIS HEIGHTS, N. Y. SARATOGA BATTLEFIELD 11
HEADQUARTERS OF GEN. ARNOLD
BENEDICT ARNOLD'S HEADQUARTERS, 1777
6A-H514

During the Battle of Saratoga General Gates and the Continental forces used this structure as a powder magazine.

Circa 1930s, $1-3

Left:
The Period House was built in 1927 on the site where Benedict Arnold had his headquarters. Both it and the Blockhouse were eventually removed.

Circa 1930s, $1-3

Using stones from the remains of the original structure and from nearby fences, the Powder Magazine was rebuilt on the same site that the original was built on.

Circa 1910s, $1-3

THE SARATOGA MONUMENT.

To commemorate the surrender of General Burgoyne and the forces under him, a group of private citizens from Saratoga County commissioned a monument to be built in the town of Victory, eight miles from the Battlefield.

Circa 1900s, $1-3

Construction began on the Saratoga Monument in 1877 and finished in 1882. It was given to the state of New York in 1895 and then to the National Park Service in 1980.

Circa 1910s, $1-3

It was near this tree on October 17, 1777, that the British Army laid down their arms and surrendered to the Continental Army. Close to 6,000 British soldiers, German mercenaries, and Iroquois and Canadian militia troops surrendered on that day.

Cancelled 1905, $1-3

SURRENDER OF BURGOYNE, SARATOGA, OCT. 17, 1777 4
48011

This camp kettle belonged to General Burgoyne and was captured from his headquarters when he surrendered.

Circa 1940s, $1-3

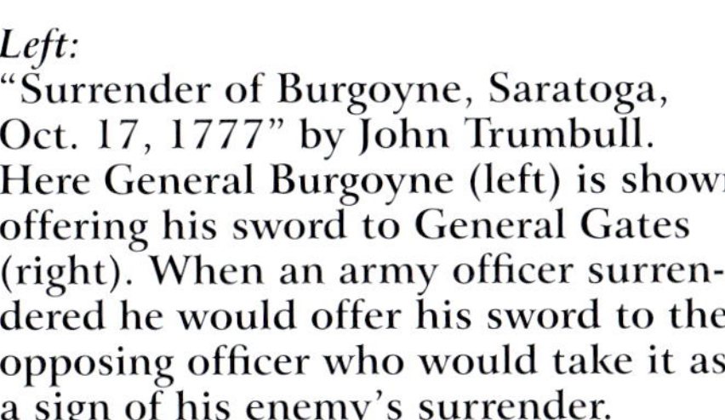

Left:
"Surrender of Burgoyne, Saratoga, Oct. 17, 1777" by John Trumbull. Here General Burgoyne (left) is shown offering his sword to General Gates (right). When an army officer surrendered he would offer his sword to the opposing officer who would take it as a sign of his enemy's surrender.

Circa 1920s, $1-3

TOP OF MIDDLE RAVINE, SARATOGA BATTLEFIELD, BEMIS HEIGHTS, N. Y.

Left:
The Middle Ravine, where British and American pickets (soldiers who are stationed away from the main body of troops to protect against surprise attack) exchanged fire between the first and second stages of the Battle.

Circa 1920s, $1-3

Some of the fiercest fighting between the British and the Americans happened along the Great Ravine.

Circa 1930s, $1-3

While leading a bayonet charge against the American position during the second part of the Battle of Saratoga, Major John Acland was shot in both legs and then captured by the advancing American forces. This obelisk marks the spot where fighting took place between General Enoch Poor's brigade (American) and forces led by Major General William Phillips (British).

Circa 1940s, $1-3

Bibliography

"A Brief History of the Canfield Casino." *Saratoga Springs History Museum.* http://www.saratoga springs-historymuseum.org/index_files/Page356. html. 6/13/06.

"And In The End…The Adelphi Hotel." *The Grand Hotels of the Victorian Era.* http://www.geocities. com/victorianlace22/index.html

"Battle of Saratoga." *Wikipedia.* http://en.wikipedia. org/wiki/Battle_of_Saratoga. 6/16/06.

Durham, Michael S. *The Smithsonian Guide to Historic America: The Mid-Atlantic States.* New York: Stewart, Tabori & Chang, 1989.

"History & Buildings: The Bathhouses." *Saratoga Spa State Park.* http://www.saratogaspastate park.org/buildinghistory_bathhouse. html. 6/16/06.

"History & Buildings: The Hall of Springs." *Saratoga Spa State Park.* http://www.saratogaspastatepark. org/buildinghistory_hall.html. 6/16/06.

"History & Buildings: Park History." *Saratoga Spa State Park.* http://www.saratogaspastatepark.org/history.html. 6/16/06.

"History & Buildings: The Victoria Pool." *Saratoga Spa State Park.* http://www.saratogaspastatepark. org/buildinghistory_pool.html. 6/16/06.

"History of the Park." *Saratoga National Historical Park.* http://www.nps.gov/sara/f-prkhst.htm. 6/16/06.

Hotaling, Edward. *They're Off!* Horse Racing at Saratoga. Syracuse: Syracuse University Press, 1995.

"In the Beginning…The Congress Hall and the Grand Union Hotel." *The Grand Hotels of the Victorian Era.* http://www.geocities.com/victorian lace22/index.html. 6/14/06.

"Saratoga Race Course." *Wikipedia.* http://en. wikipedia.org/wiki/Saratoga_Race_Course. 6/15/06.

"Saratoga Spa State Park." *Wikipedia.* http://en.wikipedia.org/wiki/Saratoga_Spa_State_ Park. 6/16/06.

"Saratoga Springs, New York." *Wikipedia.* http://en.wikipedia.org/wiki/Saratoga_Springs. 6/13/06.

"Springs: History of the Mineral Waters." *Saratoga Spa State Park.* http://www.saratogaspastatepark. org/springs.html. 6/16/06.

"Story of the Battles." *Saratoga National Historical Park.* http://www.nps.gov/sara/f-battles.htm. 6/16/06.

"The United States Hotel." *The Grand Hotels of the Victorian Era.* http://www.geocities.com/victorian lace22/UShotel.html. 6/14/06.

"Yaddo Records, 1870-1980: Historical Note." *New York Public Library Digital Library Collections.* http://digilab.nypl.org/dynaweb/ead/human/mssyaddo. 6/15/06.

Index